THE SIGHT WORD EXERCISE BOOK

READING BOOK FOR KINDERGARTEN

CHILDREN'S READING & WRITING BOOK

Speedy Publishing LLC
40 E. Main St. #1156
Newark, DE 19711
www.speedypublishing.com

RECOGNIZING
SIGHT WORDS
EXERCISES

ACTIVITY 1

Find and circle the sight words in the sentences.

SEE **HAVE** **LIKE**

1. I have a pencil.
2. I see my mom.
3. I like my friends.

ACTIVITY 2

Find and circle the sight words in the sentences.

FOR **HERE** **EAT**

1. I eat cereal everyday.
2. We live here.
3. We're going for a ride.

ACTIVITY 3

Find and circle the sight words in the sentences.

RIDE	SEE	WATER

1. I can see the rainbow.
2. My dog drinks water.
3. I like to ride my bike.

ACTIVITY 4

Find and circle the sight words in the sentences.

VAN MAP GUM

1. A map is good to have.
2. The man is in the van.
3. I bet the gum is red.

ACTIVITY 5

Find and circle the sight words in the sentences.

PET BAT HUG

1. My bat is in the bag.
2. I will hug my dad.
3. My pet is at the vet.

ACTIVITY 6

Find and circle the sight words in the sentences.

JOG	PIG	FUN

1. The pig is in the mud.
2. Can you jog with me?
3. It is fun to run.

ACTIVITY 7

Find and circle the sight words in the sentences.

PAN **MAN** **TAN**

1. The pan is black.
2. He likes to get a tan.
3. The man has a van.

ACTIVITY 8

Find and circle the sight words in the sentences.

FAN HOUR CAT

1. The cat is big.
2. We need a fan.
3. I ran for an hour.

ACTIVITY 9

Find and circle the sight words in the sentences.

BLACK CAN CAP

1. I see the black cat.
2. I can pet the dog.
3. The red cap is big.

ACTIVITY 10

Find and circle the sight words in the sentences.

BED **BROWN** **SHE**

1. The brown dog is wet.
2. His bed is blue.
3. She fed the dog.

ACTIVITY II

Find and circle the sight words in the sentences.

JET **BAG** **HOP**

1. Look at the bunny hop.
2. Do you see the jet?
3. My bag is brown.

ACTIVITY 12

Find and circle the sight words in the sentences.

BIKE **HOME** **CAKE**

1. I want to go home.
2. I like to ride my bike.
3. I want to make a cake.

ACTIVITY 13

Find and circle the sight words in the sentences.

KITE RICE GAME

1. I want to play a game.
2. I like to fly my kite.
3. I like to eat white rice.

ACTIVITY 14

Find and circle the sight words in the sentences.

DIG RED SEAL

1. My dog can dig.
2. Her lips are red.
3. I see a seal.

COLOR THE
SIGHT WORDS

ACTIVITY 15

Find and color the sight words using the code.

cat	red	fun	yellow
she	purple	the	pink

cat	fun	cat
fun	she	the
the	cat	she
fun	cat	the

ACTIVITY 16

Find and color the sight words using the code.

was	orange	are	blue
on	green	as	brown

was	are	was
as	on	on
are	was	are
on	on	as

ACTIVITY 17

Find and color the sight words using the code.

be	pink	from	green
this	orange	egg	blue

be	from	egg
this	egg	be
from	this	be
be	from	from

ACTIVITY 18

Find and color the sight words using the code.

not	purple	all	pink
but	yellow	what	orange

not	but	all
what	not	not
but	what	all
all	what	not

ACTIVITY 19

Find and color the sight words using the code.

their	yellow	do	blue
if	pink	how	brown

their	do	if
how	do	their
do	if	if
how	their	do

ACTIVITY 20

Find and color the sight words using the code.

them	red	ran	purple
then	brown	so	pink

them	then	ran
so	then	them
so	ran	so
ran	them	them

ACTIVITY 21

Find and color the sight words using the code.

has	yellow	her	orange
more	purple	two	pink

has	her	more
two	has	more
two	two	her
more	has	has

ACTIVITY 22

Find and color the sight words using the code.

make	yellow	first	green
than	pink	been	blue

make	make	than
first	been	been
than	make	first
first	than	make

ACTIVITY 23

Find and color the sight words using the code.

over 

did

down 

only

over	down	did
only	only	did
over	only	down
down	did	only

ACTIVITY 24

Find and color the sight words using the code.

big	red	very	orange
after	blue	little	green

little	very	after
big	big	little
very	after	after
little	big	after

ACTIVITY 25

Find and color the sight words using the code.

fur	pink	fly	green
sir	orange	for	blue

fur	sir	fly
for	fly	fur
sir	for	for
fly	sir	sir

ACTIVITY 26

Find and color the sight words using the code.

his	yellow	at	green
they	purple	he	pink

his	they	at
he	he	they
at	his	at
they	at	he

SIGHT WORD
SEARCH

ACTIVITY 27

Circle each sight word you find in the puzzle.

e	s	a	e	l	p
w	o	a	e	t	r
l	o	w	w	e	a
s	n	a	d	h	o
h	r	n	b	r	q
l	u	t	g	i	i

please soon want
was under

ACTIVITY 28

Circle each sight word you find in the puzzle.

l	i	s	d	d	y
g	w	h	i	t	e
o	a	w	t	m	i
o	s	e	a	l	e
d	r	c	o	e	i
p	b	l	a	c	k

black came good
pretty was white

ACTIVITY 29

Circle each sight word you find in the puzzle.

c	a	o	t	t	i
m	n	h	f	d	r
i	e	u	i	o	w
e	n	h	r	g	r
f	r	t	s	f	q
a	c	a	t	s	c

cat dog first

fun she the

ACTIVITY 30

Circle each sight word you find in the puzzle.

r	l	p	p	x	e
t	a	h	e	t	t
e	r	e	u	i	n
r	e	u	w	n	o
h	b	w	h	a	s
h	r	u	n	i	s

are	as	be
hurt	on	was

ACTIVITY 31

Circle each sight word you find in the puzzle.

h	u	x	e	n	i
i	t	n	v	g	w
i	o	e	a	i	g
b	u	t	h	i	s
m	o	r	f	e	n
n	e	t	n	h	p

but egg from
have not this

ACTIVITY 32

Circle each sight word you find in the puzzle.

n	i	w	h	a	t
d	f	y	l	h	o
g	o	l	e	f	a
d	u	i	n	c	v
a	r	p	x	r	w
a	o	e	r	r	f

all do four
if their what

ACTIVITY 33

Circle each sight word you find in the puzzle.

w	t	z	m	r	t
t	h	e	m	a	i
p	t	i	a	n	c
t	d	s	c	e	u
n	k	w	o	h	n
i	s	n	a	t	f

how	ran	so
them	then	which

ACTIVITY 34

Circle each sight word you find in the puzzle.

r	v	g	r	n	n
s	k	m	o	r	e
a	a	u	e	k	r
d	t	h	i	l	o
m	t	l	l	t	t
o	w	t	h	r	o

has	her	like
more	other	two

ACTIVITY 35

Circle each sight word you find in the puzzle.

n	a	h	t	m	t
e	e	a	s	t	i
e	i	r	r	n	i
b	k	e	i	t	s
o	v	a	f	o	o
o	b	t	m	t	e

been first its
make over than

ACTIVITY 36

Circle each sight word you find in the puzzle.

u	d	u	b	d	n
q	e	b	y	i	y
n	h	l	o	n	g
w	n	u	y	i	e
o	e	e	l	i	x
d	i	d	i	n	h

big blue did
down long only

ANSWER KEYS

Find and circle the sight words in the sentences.

SEE HAVE LIKE

1. I have a pencil.
2. I see my mom.
3. I like my friends.

Find and circle the sight words in the sentences.

FOR HERE EAT

1. I eat cereal everyday.
2. We live here.
3. We're going for a ride.

Find and circle the sight words in the sentences.

RIDE SEE WATER

1. I can see the rainbow.
2. My dog drinks water.
3. I like to ride my bike.

Find and circle the sight words in the sentences.

VAN MAP GUM

1. A map is good to have.
2. The man is in the van.
3. I bet the gum is red.

Find and circle the sight words in the sentences.

PET BAT HUG

1. My bat is in the bag.
2. I will hug my dad.
3. My pet is at the vet.

Find and circle the sight words in the sentences.

JOG PIG FUN

1. The pig is in the mud.
2. Can you jog with me.
3. It is fun to run.

Find and circle the sight words in the sentences.

PAN **MAN** **TAN**

1. The pan is black.
2. He likes to sun tan.
3. A man has a van.

Find and circle the sight words in the sentences.

FAN **HOUR** **CAT**

1. The cat is big.
2. We need a fan.
3. I ran for an hour.

Find and circle the sight words in the sentences.

BLACK CAN CAP

1. I see the black cat.
2. I can pet the dog.
3. The red cap is big.

Find and circle the sight words in the sentences.

BED BROWN SHE

1. The brown dog is wet.
2. His bed is blue.
3. She fed the dog.

Find and circle the sight words in the sentences.

JET BAG HOP

1. Look at the bunny hop.
2. Do you see the jet?
3. My bag is brown.

Find and circle the sight words in the sentences.

BIKE HOME CAKE

1. I want to go home.
2. I like to ride my bike.
3. I want to make a cake.

Find and circle the sight words in the sentences.

KITE RICE GAME

1. I want to play a game.
2. I like to fly my kite.
3. I like to eat white rice.

Find and circle the sight words in the sentences.

DIG RED SEAL

1. My dog can dig.
2. Her lips is red.
3. I see a seal.

Find and color the sight words using the code.

cat	red	fun	yellow
she	purple	the	pink

cat	fun	cat
fun	she	the
the	cat	she
fun	cat	the

Find and color the sight words using the code.

was	orange	are	blue
on	green	as	brown

was	are	was
as	on	on
are	was	are
on	on	as

Find and color the sight words using the code.

be	pink	from	green
this	orange	egg	blue

be	from	egg
this	egg	be
from	this	be
be	from	from

Find and color the sight words using the code.

not	purple	all	pink
but	yellow	what	orange

not	but	all
what	not	not
but	what	all
all	what	not

Find and color the sight words using the code.

their	do	if
how	do	their
do	if	if
how	their	do

Find and color the sight words using the code.

them	red	ran	purple
then	brown	so	pink

them	then	ran
so	then	them
so	ran	so
ran	them	them

Find and color the sight words using the code.

has	yellow	her	orange
more	purple	two	pink

has	her	more
two	has	more
two	two	her
more	has	has

Find and color the sight words using the code.

make	yellow	first	green
than	pink	been	blue

make	make	than
first	been	been
than	make	first
first	than	make

Find and color the sight words using the code.

over	purple	down	pink
did	yellow	only	orange

over	down	did
only	only	did
over	only	down
down	did	only

Find and color the sight words using the code.

big	red	very	orange
after	blue	little	green

little	very	after
big	big	little
very	after	after
little	big	after

Find and color the sight words using the code.

fur	pink	fly	green
sir	orange	for	blue

fur	sir	fly
for	fly	fur
sir	for	for
fly	sir	sir

Find and color the sight words using the code.

his	yellow	at	green
they	purple	he	pink

his	they	at
he	he	they
at	his	at
they	at	he

e	s	a	e	l	p
w	o	a	e	t	r
l	o	w	w	e	a
s	n	a	d	h	o
h	r	n	b	r	q
l	u	t	g	i	i

l	i	s	d	d	y
g	w	h	i	t	e
o	a	w	t	m	i
o	s	e	a	l	e
d	r	c	o	e	i
p	b	l	a	c	k

c	a	o	t	t	i
m	n	h	f	d	r
i	e	u	i	o	w
e	n	h	r	g	r
f	r	t	s	f	q
a	c	a	t	s	c

r	l	p	p	x	e
t	a	h	e	t	t
e	r	e	u	i	n
r	e	u	w	n	o
h	b	w	h	a	s
h	r	u	n	i	s

h	u	x	e	n	i
i	t	n	v	g	w
j	o	e	a	i	g
b	u	t	h	i	s
m	o	r	f	e	n
n	e	t	n	h	p

n	i	w	h	a	t
d	f	y	l	h	o
g	o	l	e	f	a
d	u	i	n	c	v
a	r	p	x	r	w
a	o	e	r	r	f

w	t	z	m	r	t
t	h	e	m	a	i
p	t	i	a	n	c
t	d	s	c	e	u
n	k	w	o	h	n
i	s	n	a	t	f

r	v	g	r	n	n
s	k	m	o	r	e
a	a	u	e	k	r
d	t	h	i	l	o
m	t	l	l	t	t
o	w	t	h	r	o

n a h t m t
e e a s t i
e i r r n i
b k e i t s
o v a f o o
o b t m t e

u d u b d n
q e b y i y
n h l o n g
w n u y i e
o e e l i x
d i d i n h

Visit
BABY PROFESSOR
EDUCATION KIDS
www.BabyProfessorBooks.com
to download Free Baby Professor eBooks
and view our catalog of new and exciting
Children's Books

www.ingramcontent.com/pod-product-compliance
Lightning Source LLC
LaVergne TN
LVHW060508170826
845677LV00026B/1644

* 9 7 9 8 8 6 9 4 4 1 8 7 4 *